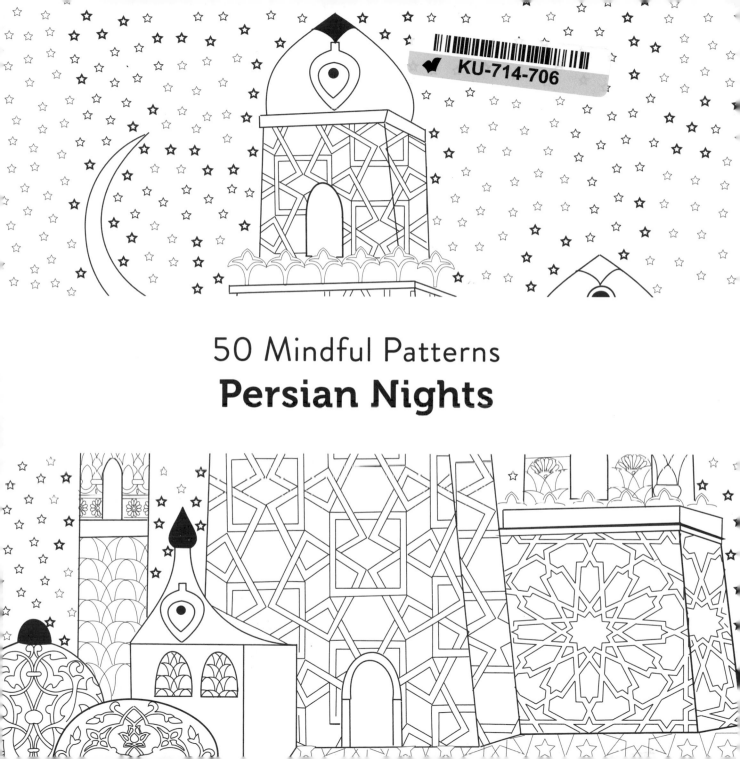

50 Mindful Patterns
Persian Nights

READER SERVICES

CUSTOMER SERVICE IN THE UK AND REPUBLIC OF IRELAND

How to continue your collection:
Subscribe online at www.50mindfulpatterns.com
UK call – 0333 300 1045; ROI call 0333 300 1046
(Calls are charged at your local rate from a landline)

Back issues: Visit our online shop at: www.hachettepartworks.com to
purchase binders, specials and any back issues you may have missed to
ensure you have a complete collection. Issues will be priced as normal with
an additional P&P cost of £1.99. Free P&P on orders over £25

CUSTOMER SERVICE, SUBSCRIPTIONS & BACK ORDERS IN OVERSEAS MARKETS

Australia - visit www.bissettmags.com.au or alternatively
call (03) 9872 4000
New Zealand - email: info@mycollectables.co.nz or alternatively
call (09) 928 4493
South Africa – visit: www.jacklin.co.za or alternatively
call (011) 265 4309

Published by Hachette Partworks Ltd, 4th Floor, Jordan House,
47 Brunswick Place, London. N1 6EB.
www.hachettepartworks.com

Editorial and Design by Wonderland Collective
Pattern Designs by Hachette Pratique

Distributed in the UK and Republic Of Ireland by Marketforce.
Copyright 2016 Hachette Partworks Ltd

Printed in the European Union.
ISSN: 2398-1954
ALL RIGHTS RESERVED

The editor's policy is to use papers that are natural, renewable and
recyclable products and made from wood grown in sustainable forests.
The logging and manufacturing processes are expected to conform
to the environmental regulations of the country of origin.

MAGIC AND MYSTERY;
IMAGINATION AND DREAMS

Persian Nights takes you back to the magic and
mystery of ancient Persia; to dark desert nights
and magnificent turrets silhouetted against deep
orange sun sets.

In the much-loved stories of One Thousand and
One Nights, Scheherazade captivated the king
of Persia with her exotic tales. In the same way,
we hope that this book will mèsmerise you, as you
trace the intricate patterns on each page, filling
them with the rich colours of a golden age.

Life's twists can lead you
to true beauty. But to see
it, you must first open
your eyes.

"When you do things from
your soul, you feel a river
moving in you, a joy."
- Rumi

How will your soul mate
find you if you blend into
the crowd?

Look up. See the universe
of stars pin-pricking the
velvet indigo sky.

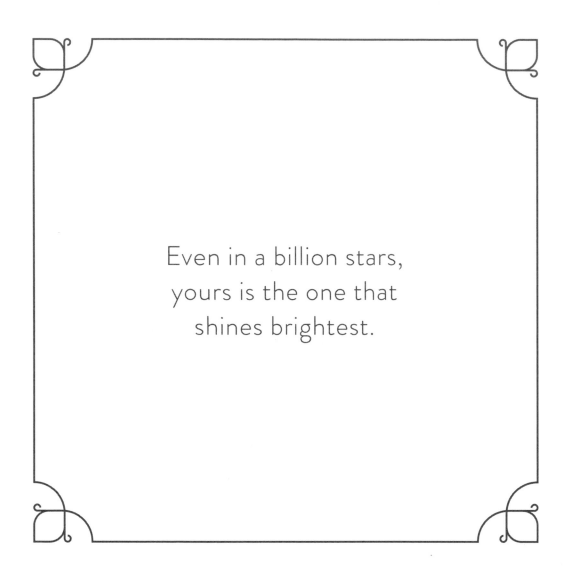

Even in a billion stars,
yours is the one that
shines brightest.

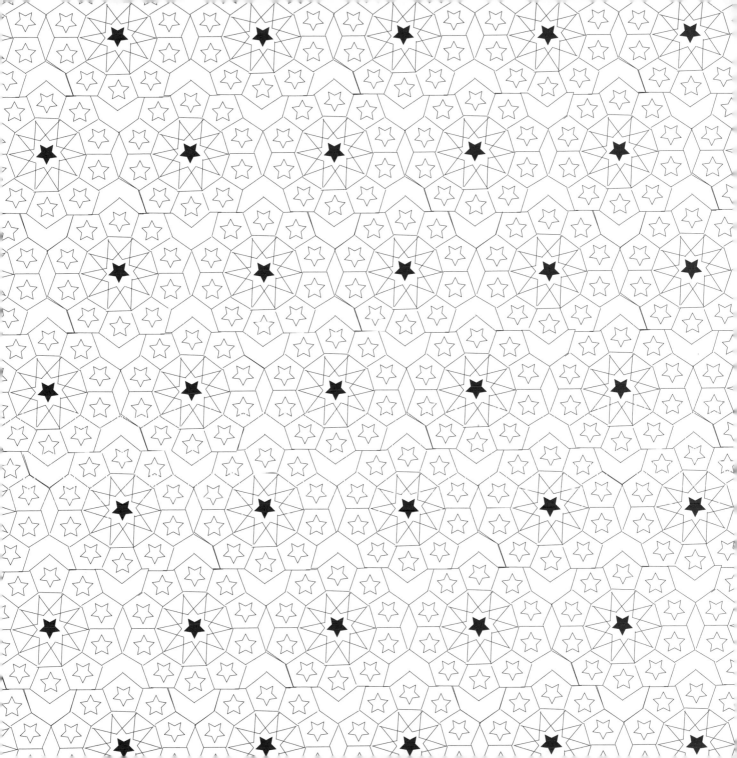

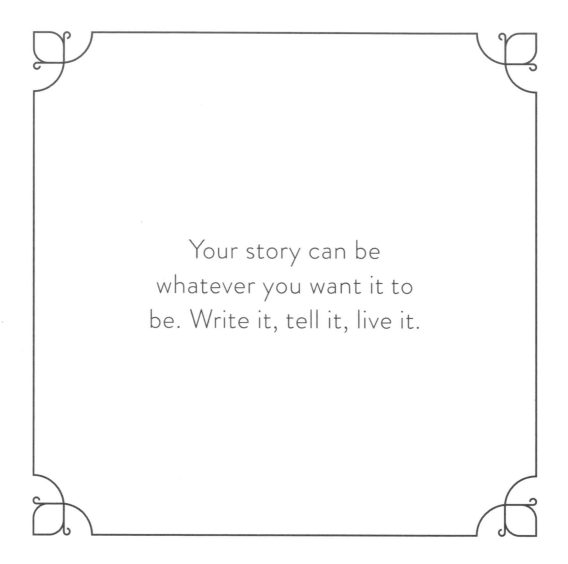

Your story can be
whatever you want it to
be. Write it, tell it, live it.

"Dance less in motion and more in spirit; awaken the dreamer within."
– Shah Asad Rizvi

Everything in this world
is connected. That's how
love is shared.

You are your own song.
Sing it loud!

Life's chaos can
be overwhelming.
Remember to breathe.

If you shift your focus,
even slightly, it becomes
possible to see a new
perspective.

A beautiful oasis can
thrive even in the most
arid desert.

Look beyond the façade
to reveal the truth that
lies within.

It's not always about
reaching a destination.
Rather, it's about the path
you take to get there.

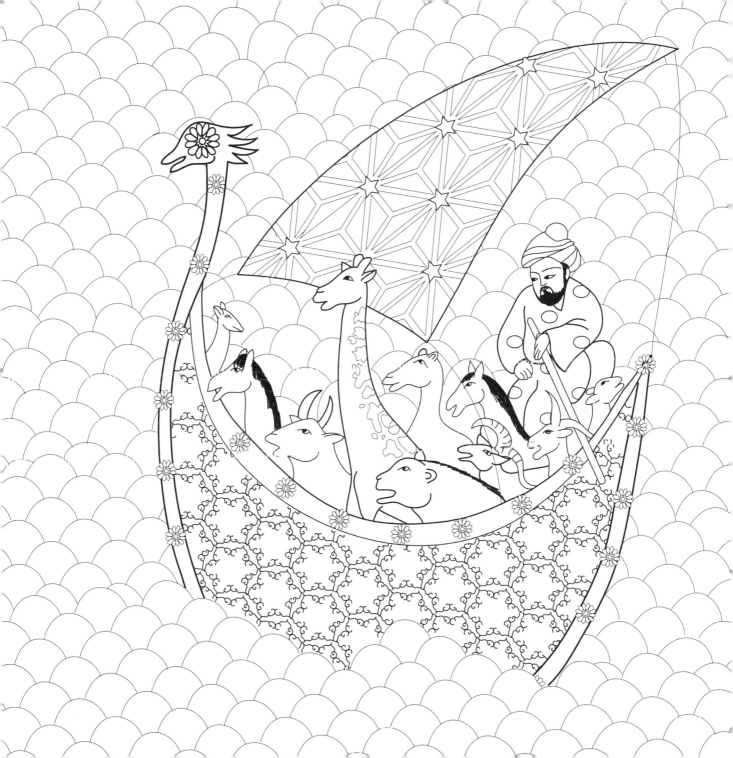

Breathe consciously to
calm your restless mind.

Savour the joy of giving.

Feel love. Be kind.
Show compassion.

"Respond to every call
that excites your spirit."
– Rumi

The only rules that bind
your life are the ones you
make yourself.

Show your true colours!
They are truly dazzling.

Colours flow from your
mind like a river of
crystal water.

The differences around
you enrich your journey
through life.

Celebrate your life.
It's the only one you have.
Be joyful!

There can be profound
beauty in simplicity.

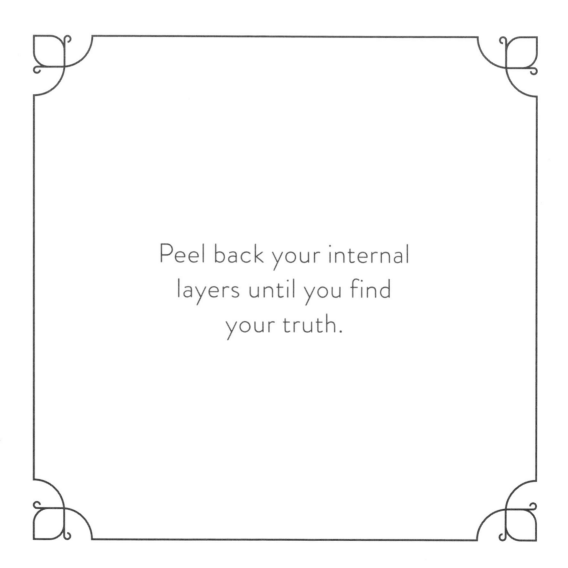

Peel back your internal
layers until you find
your truth.

As life pulls you all
directions, remember
to focus on the single
essence that is you.

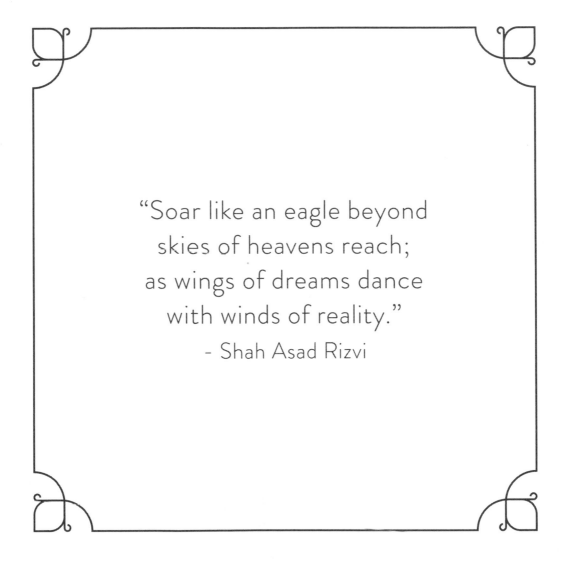

"Soar like an eagle beyond
skies of heavens reach;
as wings of dreams dance
with winds of reality."
- Shah Asad Rizvi

Fuel the flames of your
spirit with love.

Follow the crescent moon.
It will guide you in your
darkest hour.

Every experience expands
your understanding of the
world's mysteries.

Trace the intricate
patterns of beauty with
a quiet mind.

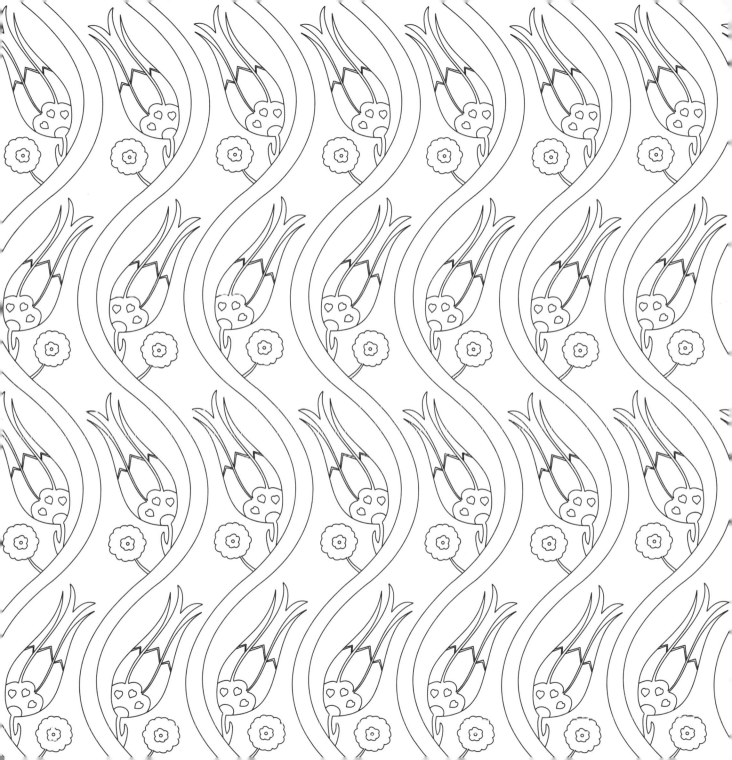

Tears can cleanse your
troubled thoughts.
Let them flow.

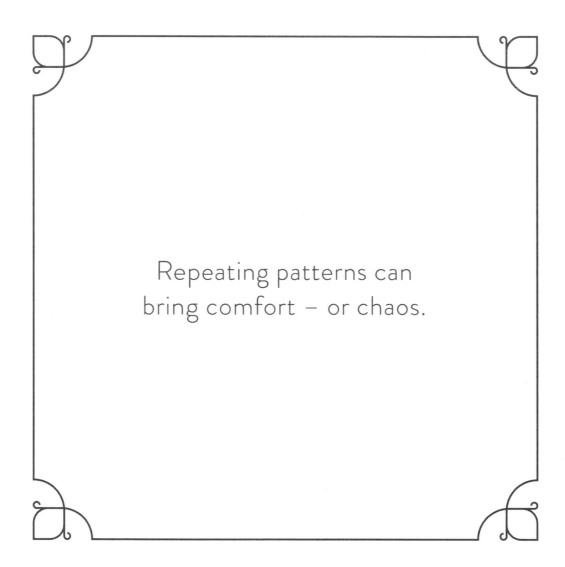

Repeating patterns can
bring comfort – or chaos.

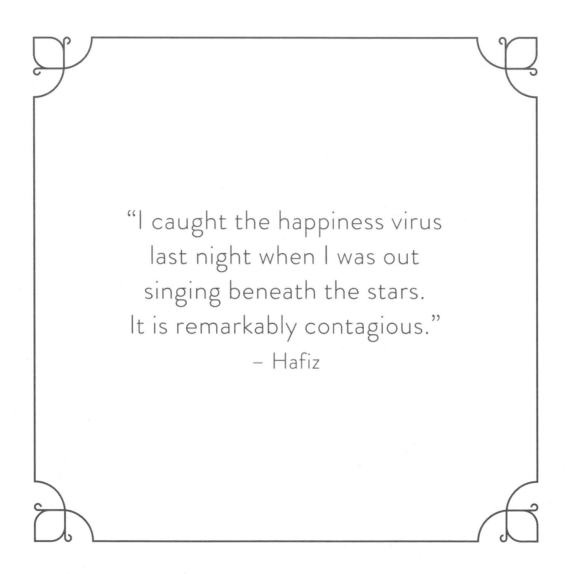

"I caught the happiness virus
last night when I was out
singing beneath the stars.
It is remarkably contagious."
– Hafiz

You have infinite
power to bloom.

Let your beautiful
light shine every day,
in every way.

You can only truly hear
when you are silent.
Listen.

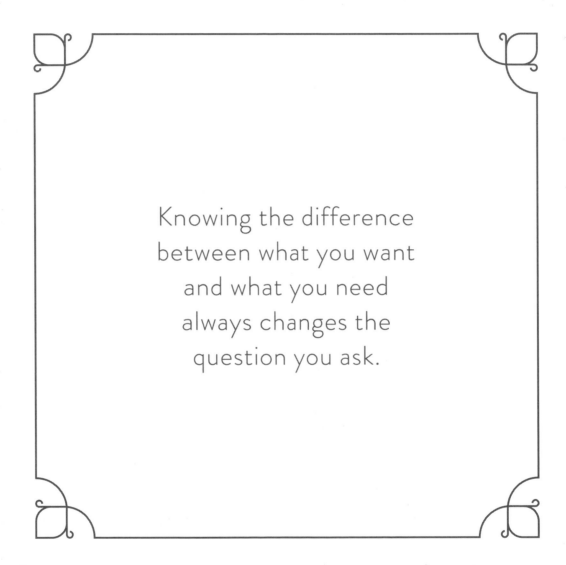

Knowing the difference
between what you want
and what you need
always changes the
question you ask.

Set boundaries, not limits.

If you want to grow,
you must first plant
seeds in fertile ground.

"For I have learned that
every heart will get what
it prays for most."
- Hafiz

Open the window and
inhale the fresh fragrance
of the world before dawn.

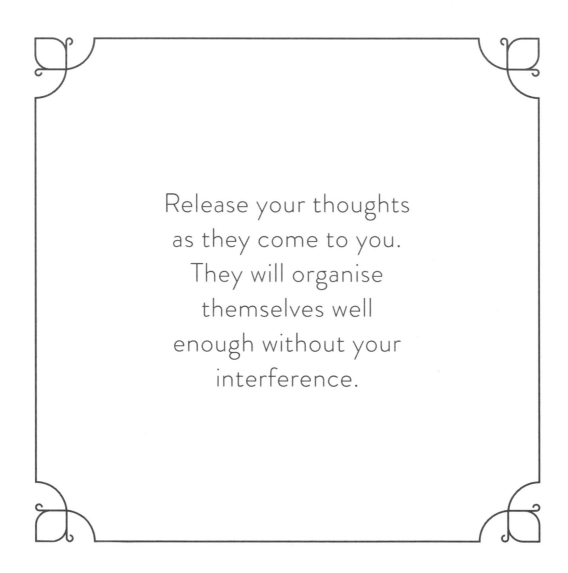

Release your thoughts
as they come to you.
They will organise
themselves well
enough without your
interference.

Let your fears go, and
watch them softly land like
confetti in a storm.

✄ Cut these patterns to make your own bookmarks.
Once cut you can paste them back to back.

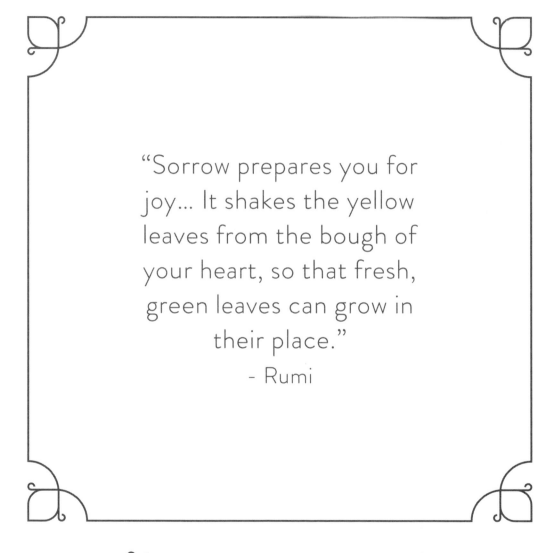

"Sorrow prepares you for joy... It shakes the yellow leaves from the bough of your heart, so that fresh, green leaves can grow in their place."
– Rumi

✂ Cut these patterns to make your own bookmarks.
Once cut you can paste them back to back.

All roads in your life lead
to your unique centre.
That's your ultimate
destination.

✂ Cut these patterns to make your own bookmarks.
Once cut you can paste them back to back.

LOOK OUT FOR MORE BEAUTIFUL BOOKS

ART THERAPY
50 Mindful Patterns
**Under
the Sea**
5

ART THERAPY
50 Mindful Patterns
**All the Fun
of the Fair**
6